At the
Zoo

by **Dana Meachen Rau**

Reading Consultant: Nanci R. Vargus, Ed.D.

Marshall Cavendish
Benchmark
New York

Picture Words

animals

ball

chimpanzee

elephant

feathers

giraffe

 leaf

peacock

 rock

 sea lion

 snake

tree

Look at the in the zoo!

Look at the lift its trunk.

Look at the  fan its .

Look at the  eat a 🍁.

Look at the  rest under a .

Look at the  play with a 🏐.

Look at the  climb a .

Look at me climb like a !

Looking at is fun.

Words to Know

climb (klime)
   to go up something to get higher

fan
   to spread out

lift
   to bring something higher

Find Out More

Books

Hoena, B. A. *The Zoo*. Mankato, MN: Capstone Press, 2004.

LeBoutillier, Nate. *A Day in the Life of a Zookeeper*. Mankato, MN: Capstone Press, 2005.

Zoehfeld, Kathleen Weidner. *Wild Lives: A History of the People and Animals of the Bronx Zoo*. New York: Alfred A. Knopf, 2006.

Videos

Balaban, Larry. *A Trip to the San Diego Zoo*. Genius Products, 2004.

Stein, Garth. *A Day at the Zoo*. Katzfilms.

Web Sites

Bronx Zoo
http://www.bronxzoo.com/

San Diego Zoo
http://www.sandiegozoo.org/

Smithsonian National Zoological Park
http://nationalzoo.si.edu/

About the Author

Dana Meachen Rau is an author, editor, and illustrator. A graduate of Trinity College in Hartford, Connecticut, she has written more than one hundred books for children, including nonfiction, biographies, early readers, and historical fiction. She likes go to the Beardsley Zoo in Connecticut with her children.

About the Reading Consultant

Nanci R. Vargus, Ed.D., wants all children to enjoy reading. She used to teach first grade. Now she works at the University of Indianapolis. Nanci helps young people become teachers. The Cincinnati Zoo is a favorite place to go with granddaughters Corinne and Charlotte.

Marshall Cavendish Benchmark
99 White Plains Road
Tarrytown, NY 10591-9001
www.marshallcavendish.us

Library of Congress Cataloging-in-Publication Data

Rau, Dana Meachen, 1971–
At the zoo / by Dana Meachen Rau.
    p. cm. — (Benchmark rebus)
Summary: Introduces various animals at the zoo through simple text with rebuses.
Includes bibliographical references.
ISBN-13: 978-0-7614-2610-3
1. Rebuses. [1. Zoo animals—Fiction. 2. Zoos—Fiction. 3. Rebuses.] I. Title.
PZ7.R193975At 2007
[E]—dc22
        2006023244

Editor: Christine Florie
Publisher: Michelle Bisson
Art Director: Anahid Hamparian
Series Designer: Virginia Pope

Photo research by Connie Gardner

Rebus images, with the exception of the chimpanzee, provided courtesy of *Dorling Kindersley*.

Cover photo by Frank Pedrick/The Image Works

The photographs in this book are used with permission and through the courtesy of:
Pinto/zefa/CORBIS: p. 2 (chimpanzee); *Photo Researchers*: p. 5 Mark Newman; p. 7 Will and Deni McIntyre; p. 13 Larry Miller; *Minden Pictures*: p. 9 Tui De Roy; *Corbis*: p. 11 Yann Arthus-Bertrand; p. 15 Chris Collins; p. 21 Gerald French; *Jupiter Images*: p. 17 Oxford Scientific; *Alamy*: p. 19 John Terence Turner.

Printed in Malaysia
1 3 5 6 4 2